SCATALOG
A Kid's Field Guide to Animal Poop

HOW TO TRACK
A RHINOCEROS

Dory Zane

"BECAUSE EVERYBODY POOPS"

WINDMILL
BOOKS
New York

Published in 2014 by Windmill Books, An Imprint of Rosen Publishing
29 East 21st Street, New York, NY 10010

First Edition

Editor: Amelie von Zumbusch
Photo Research: Katie Stryker
Book Design: Colleen Bialecki

Photo Credits: Cover (top) Francois Loubser/Shutterstock.com; cover (bottom) TJ/Flickr; background Ginger Livingston Sanders/Shutterstock.com; p. 5 Scott Ward/Shutterstock.com; p. 6 Stacey Ann Alberts/ Shutterstock.com; p. 8 Jan Damkjaer; p. 9 JacoBecker/Shutterstock.com; p. 11 Francois van Heerden/ Shutterstock.com; p. 12 Pal Teravagimov/Shutterstock.com; p. 13 Four Oaks/Shutterstock.com; p. 15 nelik/ Shutterstock.com; pp. 16, 18 Elise Ney/Flickr; p. 17 iStockphoto/Shutterstock.com; p. 19 Lorimer Images/ Shutterstock.com; p. 21 John Warburton-Lee/AWL Images/Getty Images; p. 22 Albie Venter/Shutterstock.com.

Library of Congress Cataloging-in-Publication Data

Zane, Dory.
  How to track a rhinoceros / by Dory Zane. — First edition.
    pages cm. — (Scatalog: a kid's field guide to animal poop)
Includes index.
  ISBN 978-1-61533-886-3 (library) — ISBN 978-1-61533-892-4 (pbk.) —
ISBN 978-1-61533-898-6 (6-pack)
  1. Rhinoceroses—Juvenile literature. 2. Animal droppings—Juvenile literature. I. Title.
QL737.U63.Z36 2014
599.66'8—dc23
                            2013026698

Manufactured in the United States of America

CPSIA Compliance Information: Batch # BW14WM: For Further Information contact Windmill Books, New York, New York at 1-866-478-0556

CONTENTS

TRACKING RHINOCEROSES

The rhinoceros is Earth's second-largest land mammal, after the elephant. Rhinoceroses are known for their thick skin and large horns. There are five living species of rhinoceroses. Three species live in Asia, while two are **native** to Africa. The African rhinoceroses are the white rhino and the black rhino. Both the white rhino and the black rhino have two horns.

Black rhinos are also known as hooked-lip rhinos. They can eat about 50 pounds (23 kg) of food each day. That produces lots of poop!

HOW TO TELL BLACK AND WHITE RHINOS APART

BLACK RHINOS

○ 4.5–5.5 feet (1.4–1.7 m) tall, at shoulder

Tracks

○ 9–10 inches (23–25 cm) long

WHITE RHINOS

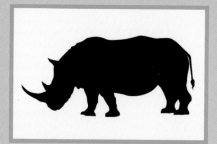

○ 5–6 feet (1.5–1.8 m) tall, at shoulder

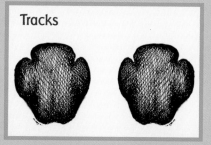
Tracks

○ 10–11 inches (25–28 cm) long

Trackers use several clues to tell black and white rhinos apart. White rhinos are bigger. They also have bigger and somewhat differently shaped tracks.

You can learn a lot about rhinos by tracking them. Wildlife groups track rhinos to keep them safe from **poachers**. One great, if gross, way to track rhinos is to examine their poop, or dung! Poop can tell us a lot about rhinos.

WHERE TO FIND RHINOS

Black rhinos and white rhinos once had a very large **range**. However, the number of wild rhinos in Africa has gotten much smaller over time. Black rhinos have died out in western Africa. White rhinos in northern Africa are extremely rare.

These white rhinos are grazing on a savanna in Kenya's Lake Nakuru National Park. Savannas are grassy plains with few trees.

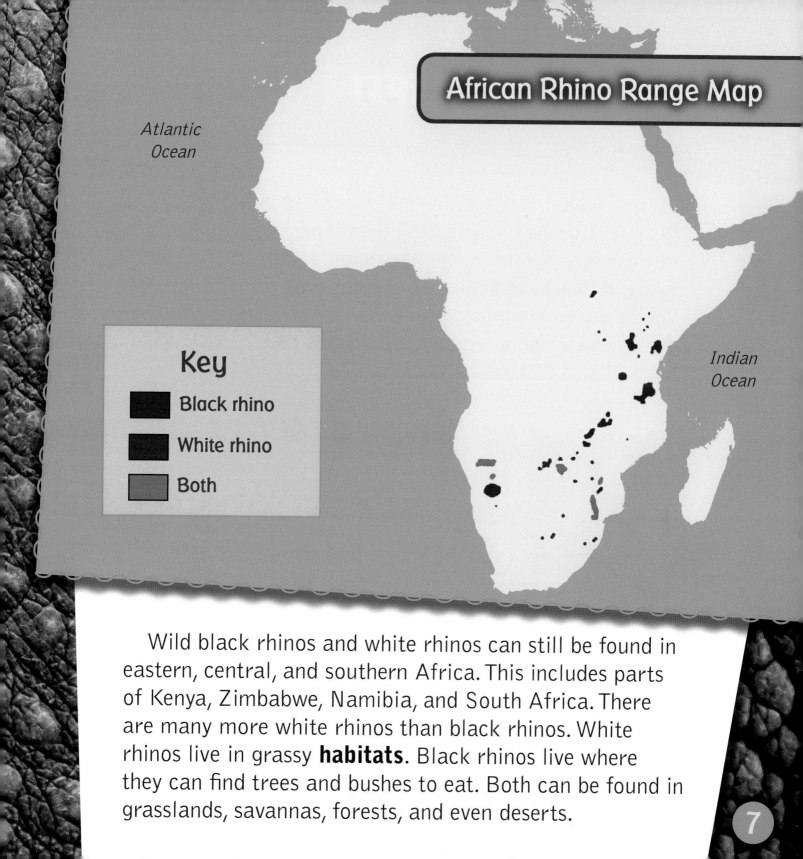

African Rhino Range Map

Atlantic
Ocean

Indian
Ocean

Key

Black rhino

White rhino

Both

Wild black rhinos and white rhinos can still be found in eastern, central, and southern Africa. This includes parts of Kenya, Zimbabwe, Namibia, and South Africa. There are many more white rhinos than black rhinos. White rhinos live in grassy **habitats**. Black rhinos live where they can find trees and bushes to eat. Both can be found in grasslands, savannas, forests, and even deserts.

LOOK AT THE LIPS!

Both white rhinos and black rhinos are actually gray in color. However, you can tell them apart by the shape of their lips! White rhinos have wide, square-shaped lips. Black rhinos have hooked upper lips that come to a point. White rhinos are much larger than black rhinos. White rhinos can weigh almost 8,000 pounds (3,629 kg), while black rhinos can weigh 3,000 pounds (1,361 kg).

This is a white rhino. Rhinos can be dangerous if you get too close. Smart trackers are always careful.

Rhinos' thick skin protects them from predators, prickly thorns, and sharp grasses. Although they are hard, rhinos' horns are not made of bone. Instead, they are made of **keratin**, as human nails and hair are.

This is a black rhino. The front horn is the longer one on both black rhinos and white rhinos. Rhino horns can grow as much as 3 inches (8 cm) each year.

9

RHINOS' LIVES

Black rhinos are mostly solitary as adults. They each have their own **territories**. White rhinos are social animals. They often live in groups, called herds or crashes. Up to 15 white rhinos may form a herd. Herds are made up mostly of female rhinos and their babies. Male white rhinos are territorial, as are black rhinos.

During the day, rhinos' habitats can be very hot and sunny. Rhinos rest in the shade to stay cool. They also **wallow** in water holes and cover their skin with mud. Mud acts like sunblock for rhinos. It also keeps insects from biting them.

Rhinos often leave trails of muddy tracks after they climb out of mud holes like this one. Trackers sometimes follow these trails to find rhinos.

RHINO BABIES

Male and female rhinos **mate** throughout the year. Males can tell when a female rhino is ready to mate by smelling her urine and dung. Female rhinos give birth about 16 months after mating. They have one baby at a time.

Rhino mothers keep a close watch over their calves and will defend them whenever needed.

Baby rhinos produce smaller tracks and dung than adults do. Trackers use tracks and poop size to guess the age of the rhino that left it.

Baby rhinos are called calves. A calf can stand up about an hour after it is born. Calves follow their mothers everywhere. At first, they drink just her milk. After two months, they also start eating plants. Calves stay with their mothers for about three years, at which point mothers are ready to have another baby.

POOPING PLANT PIECES

Rhinos are herbivores. This means they eat only plants. White rhinos eat mostly grasses. Their wide mouths are perfect for **grazing**. Black rhinos eat from trees and bushes. They use their pointed upper lips to grab twigs, leaves, and fruits from branches.

RHINO DIGESTIVE SYSTEM

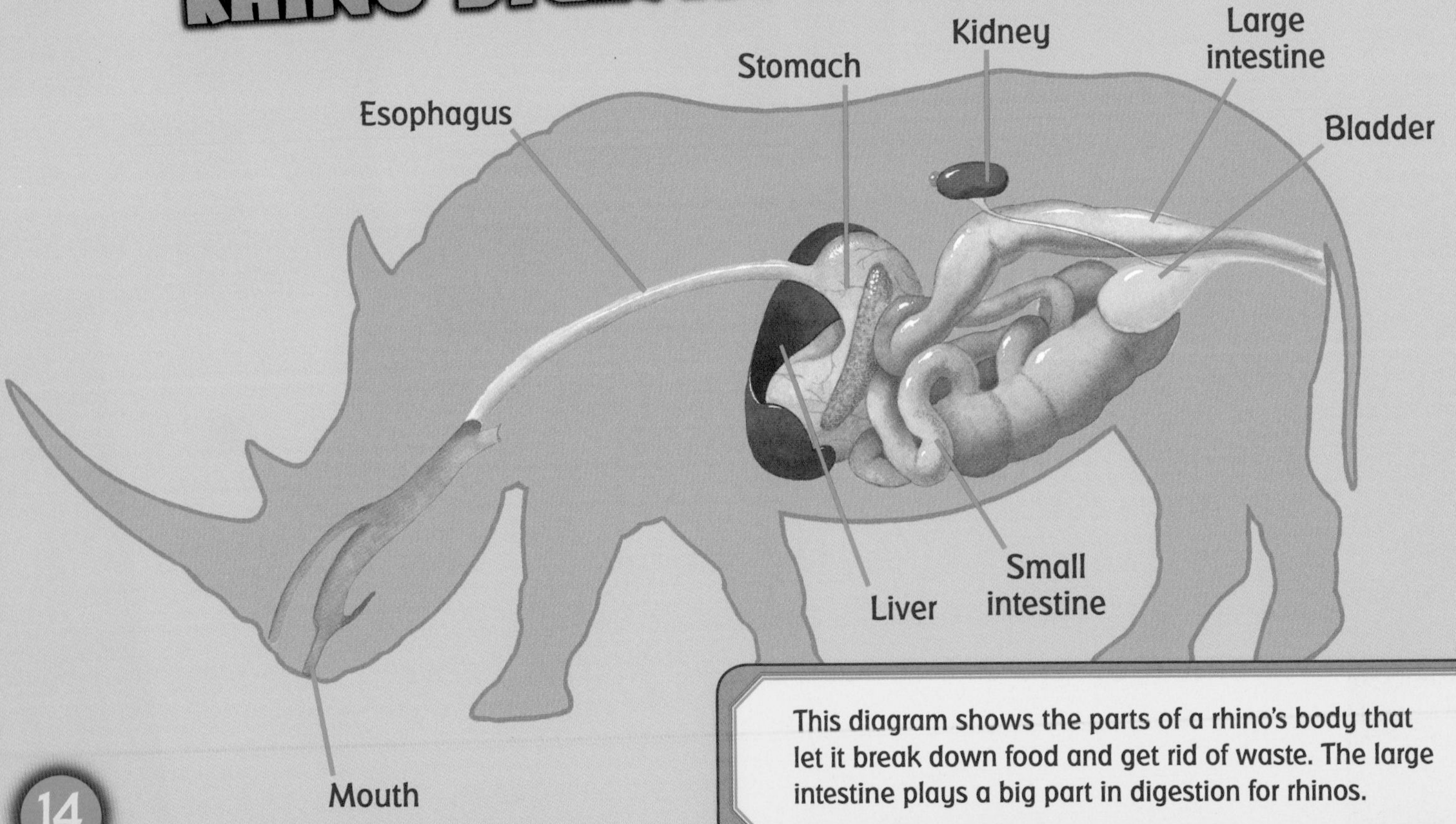

Esophagus

Stomach

Kidney

Large intestine

Bladder

Liver

Small intestine

Mouth

This diagram shows the parts of a rhino's body that let it break down food and get rid of waste. The large intestine plays a big part in digestion for rhinos.

Since the plants that rhinos eat are hard to digest, rhinos make a lot of waste. For example, white rhinos tend to poop five or six times a day.

Black rhinos and white rhinos do not have teeth in the fronts of their mouths. They grind up their food with powerful flat teeth in the backs of their mouths. Plants are hard to **digest**. This means that if you look at rhino poop, you will see what they have been eating. Rhino poop is full of pieces of grass, twigs, or leaves.

PILES OF DUNG!

Black rhinos and white rhinos leave their dung in piles, called middens. Pooping in a dung pile helps rhinos leave messages for each other. Every rhino's poop has its own smell. By smelling the dung pile, rhinos can tell a lot about other nearby rhinos. This includes whether they are young or old and if they are male or female.

This is a rhinoceros midden. Rhinos will sometimes shuffle their feet through a midden after adding their own poop to it.

A rhinoceros's great sense of smell means that it is able to discover things about other rhinos in the area by smelling their poop.

Dung piles may mark a rhino's territory. Rhinos also spray their territories with urine. When a male sprays his urine, it tells other males to stay away. When a female sprays her urine, it tells males whether or not she is ready to mate.

WHAT CAN DUNG TELL YOU?

A safari is a trip on which people look at animals. Safari trackers locate animals for visitors to look at. Trackers use dung piles to track rhinos. When all the dung in a pile is old, trackers know that rhinos have moved out of an area. If there is new dung in the pile, it is likely that rhinos are nearby.

RHINO POOP

Bits of grass

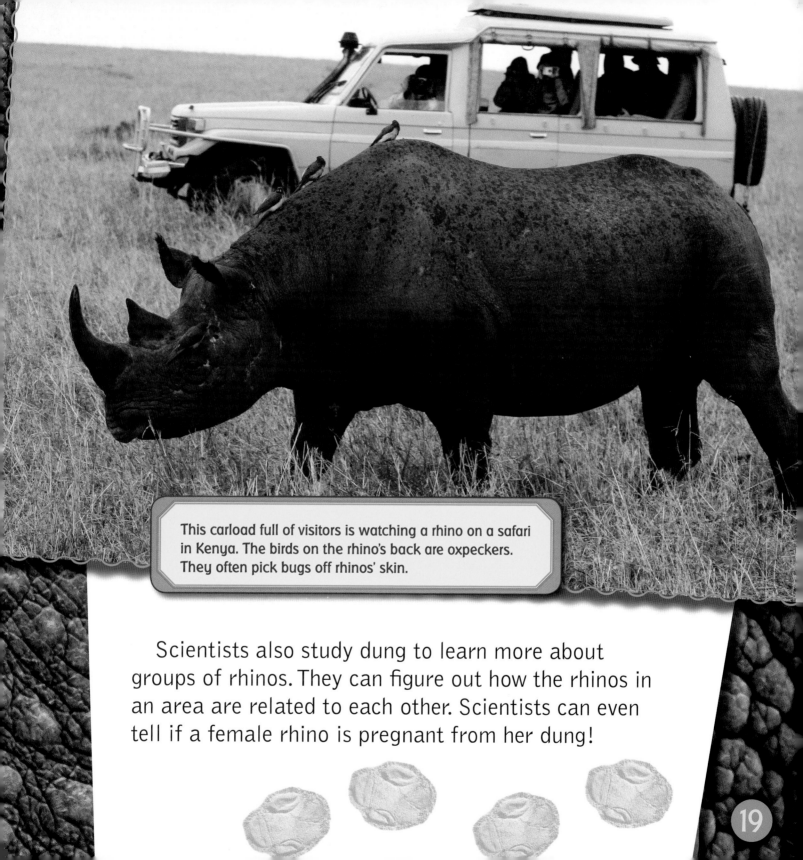

This carload full of visitors is watching a rhino on a safari in Kenya. The birds on the rhino's back are oxpeckers. They often pick bugs off rhinos' skin.

Scientists also study dung to learn more about groups of rhinos. They can figure out how the rhinos in an area are related to each other. Scientists can even tell if a female rhino is pregnant from her dung!

KEEPING RHINOS SAFE

Both white rhinos and black rhinos are in danger of dying out. In fact, during the last 100 years, Earth's rhinos almost became **extinct**! Hunters killed rhinos to sell their horns. Before 1900, more than 500,000 rhinos lived in Africa and Asia. Today, there are just 20,000 white rhinos and 5,000 black rhinos left in the wild.

Wildlife-conservation groups in Africa have helped save rhinos from dying out. They track rhinos and help keep them safe from poachers. Many rhinos live in wildlife sanctuaries and national parks. These include the Mkomazi Rhino Sanctuary, in Tanzania, and the Hluhluwe-iMfolozi Park, in South Africa.

These white rhinos are in Spioenkop Nature Reserve, in KwaZulu Natal, South Africa.

THE FUTURE FOR RHINOS

Many trackers work with wildlife groups, national parks, and wildlife sanctuaries. They help scientists figure out how many rhinos live in an area. Some trackers even use their skills to find and stop rhino poachers.

In the 1890s, there were less than 100 wild white rhinos. Today, there are more white rhinos than any other rhino species. However, black rhinos are now **critically endangered**. People need to work together to keep rhinos safe from dying out!

These are white rhinos. White rhinos may live for around 50 years. Black rhinos can live for about 35 years in the wild.

GLOSSARY

critically endangered (KRIH-tih-kuh-lee in-DAYN-jerd) Very close to dying out.

digest (dy-JEST) To break down food so that the body can use it.

extinct (ik-STINGKT) No longer existing.

grazing (GRAY-zing) Feeding on grass.

habitats (HA-buh-tats) The kinds of land where animals or plants naturally live.

keratin (KER-uh-tun) Matter that is found in people's hair and nails and in animal fur, scales, and horns.

mammal (MA-mul) A warm-blooded animal that has a backbone and hair, breathes air, and feeds milk to its young.

mate (MAYT) To come together to make babies.

native (NAY-tiv) Born or grown in a certain place or country.

poachers (POH-cherz) People who illegally kill animals that are protected by the law.

range (RAYNJ) The place in which a kind of animal can be found.

territories (TER-uh-tor-eez) Land or space that animals guard for their use.

wallow (WAH-loh) To roll around in mud or muddy water.

INDEX

WEBSITES

For web resources related to the subject of this book, go to:
www.windmillbooks.com/weblinks and select this book's title.